MILLARD FILLMORE

OUR THIRTEENTH PRESIDENT

by Gerry and Janet Souter

THE CHILD'S WORLD®

PUBLISHED IN THE UNITED STATES OF AMERICA

THE CHILD'S WORLD®
1980 Lookout Drive • Mankato, MN 56003-1705
800-599-READ • www.childsworld.com

ACKNOWLEDGMENTS
The Child's World®: Mary Berendes, Publishing Director

Creative Spark: Mary McGavic, Project Director; Melissa McDaniel, Editorial
Director, Deborah Goodsite, Photo Research

The Design Lab: Kathleen Petelinsek, Design; Gregory Lindholm, Page Production

Content Adviser: David R. Smith, Adjunct Assistant Professor of History,
University of Michigan–Ann Arbor

PHOTOS
Cover and page 3: White House Historical Association (White House Collection),
(detail); White House Historical Association (White House Collection)

Interior: Alamy: 6 (The Print Collector); The Art Archive: 23 (Culver Pictures);
Art Resource, NY: 22 (National Portrait Gallery, Smithsonian Institution), 32
(The New York Public Library); The Bridgeman Art Library: 12 (Musee du Grand
Orient de France, Paris, France/Archives Charmet), 13 (Private Collection/Ken
Welsh), 26 (Hirshhorn Museum, Washington D.C., USA); Courtesy of the Buffalo
and Erie County Historical Society: 19, 28, 33, 34, 36; Corbis: 5 and 38 (Lee
Snider/Photo Images), 10, 17 and 38 (Bettmann); Getty Images: 21 and 39 (MPI);
The Granger Collection, New York: 8, 24, 30; iStockphoto: 44 (Tim Fan); Library
of Congress: 4, 20, 35, 37 and 39; SuperStock: 15, 31 (SuperStock, Inc.), 16
(Stock Montage); U.S. Air Force photo: 45.

LIBRARY OF CONGRESS CATALOGING–IN–PUBLICATION DATA
Souter, Gerry.
   Millard Fillmore / by Gerry and Janet Souter.
      p. cm. — (Presidents of the U.S.A.)
   Includes bibliographical references and index.
   ISBN 978–1–60253–042–3 (library bound : alk. paper)
   1. Fillmore, Millard, 1800–1874—Juvenile literature. 2. Presidents—United
States—Biography—Juvenile literature. I. Souter, Janet, 1940– II. Title.
   E427.S67 2008
   973.6'4092—dc22
   [B]

                                                2007049063

*Millard Fillmore
in a portrait by
George P. A. Healy*

TABLE OF CONTENTS

FROM POVERTY TO LEADERSHIP

Millard Fillmore began life as a poor farmer's son. From this desperate background, he would rise to the peak of power, becoming the 13th president of the United States.

Fillmore was born in a one-room log cabin in Cayuga County, New York, on January 7, 1800, the second of eight children. His father, Nathaniel, was barely able to scratch a living from the ground. Nathaniel and his wife, Phoebe, loved their son very much. They wanted him to have a better life. At the age of 14, they sent Millard to work as an **apprentice** at a cloth mill. There he would learn the craft of cloth making.

In those days, an apprentice agreed to work for very low pay for a certain length of time in

Millard Fillmore had a reputation for being honorable and hardworking.

order to learn a skill. To leave early, apprentices had to pay money to the boss as a penalty for not staying as long as they had promised.

To Millard Fillmore, the apprenticeship felt more like slavery. He hated the work, and the cruel mill boss sometimes beat his workers. Fillmore saved what little

This cabin is a replica of Millard Fillmore's birthplace. Fillmore was born in a log cabin near Moravia, in west-central New York.

A young boy helps prepare cotton to be carded. Millard Fillmore worked in a carding mill as a boy.

money he made. He paid the penalty that allowed him to leave early. Then he walked 100 miles back to his family's little cabin.

Fillmore's father refused to give up on his son's future. He sent Millard to work in a carding mill, where sheep's wool was untangled and spun into thread. The owner of this mill was a kind man. Fillmore learned to like the work. While tending the carding machines, he kept an open dictionary nearby. He would take a few minutes here and there to learn new words. He later remembered that he had been "determined to seek out the meaning of every word . . . which I did not understand" and "fix it in my memory."

At age 16, Fillmore began attending a one-room school. A year later, using what little money he had, he subscribed to a circulating library. The library charged a small fee in exchange for loaning books to readers. Later, a teacher in a nearby village started a school called the New Hope Academy. Fillmore enrolled and went to classes whenever he could leave the mill.

By 1819, 19-year-old Millard Fillmore was a handsome, strapping young man of six feet tall. He was in love with Abigail Powers, a 21-year-old teacher. She respected his ambition and his desire for education. But Fillmore was the son of a poor farmer. Abigail was an intelligent, well-read clergyman's daughter. He wanted to improve his position in life before even thinking of marriage. Although his apprenticeship still had two more years to go, he again paid the penalty money to leave the mill early. Nathaniel Fillmore supported his son's ambition.

The Fillmore family moved to Montville, New York, where Nathaniel became a tenant farmer for Judge Walter Wood. This meant that Nathaniel farmed land for the judge. He received either some of the crop

Millard Fillmore was the first president born in the 19th century.

Abigail Powers began teaching when she was 16 years old to help support her widowed mother.

Books were scarce and expensive in backwoods areas of the early 19th century. A circulating library was a collection of books put together by a group of readers. They subscribed to the library by paying a small sum of money. The library bought books using the subscription money or funds donated by subscribers.

FROM POVERTY TO LEADERSHIP

Buffalo, New York, was a small but growing city when Millard Fillmore moved there in the 1820s.

or a small amount of money in return. In a short time, Nathaniel persuaded the judge to take on Millard as an apprentice clerk in his law office.

Millard Fillmore was typical of many young men who wanted to become lawyers. Law firms employed many young men as clerks. All legal papers had to be copied by hand and then taken to a printer to be set in type, so law clerks had to know how to read and write. They also had to know where legal information was found in a law library.

Millard Fillmore faced a seven-year apprenticeship. Once again, he was tied to a difficult and cruel employer. Fillmore longed to be his own man. His ambition drove him to take a teaching job to earn extra

8

money. Then he bought out the rest of his apprenticeship so the judge would instead give him full pay for his work. Fillmore and Judge Wood did not get along. After they had a bitter argument, Fillmore resigned. Brokenhearted, he returned to working the plow on the family farm. Many years later, Fillmore remembered this part of his life: "It made me feel for the weak and unprotected and to hate the insolent tyrant in any station in life."

Fillmore was desperate to achieve something with his life. He journeyed to the growing town of Buffalo, New York, on the shores of Lake Erie. In the 1820s, Buffalo was not a large city. Only about 2,400 people called it home. In 1804, a land agent named Joseph Ellicott had designed a spoked-wheel street grid for Buffalo. It was one of only three cities in the United States with that sort of design. Buffalo's streets were dirt with raised wood sidewalks. A new courthouse had been built by 1816. Fillmore's arrival could not have been better timed. In 1817, New York governor DeWitt Clinton had convinced New York lawmakers to fund the 363-mile Erie Canal. Buffalo was ready for major growth.

In 1822, Fillmore began working for a law firm as a clerk. It usually took a person seven years to train for the law. Fillmore completed his studies in two years through the sheer force of his will. He impressed his fellow workers as he continued to teach school and study law at the same time. At the recommendation of his employers, Fillmore began to practice law.

Law schools were rare in Fillmore's time. Few young people could afford law school or the many books that were needed. Most lawyers in the West or in backwoods communities learned by reading law books on the job while they worked as low-paid clerks in law firms. This type of study was called "reading law."

Abigail Powers Fillmore loved books and learning. She worked as a teacher for a time, and later she and her husband helped start a library in Buffalo.

In the 1820s, education beyond basic reading and writing was rare for young women. Abigail Powers Fillmore had been taught at home by her mother using materials from her father's library.

Fillmore's early struggles shaped him into a hard-working, determined man. He would always fight for the underdog, having been one himself for so many years. He worked to hold on to what he had achieved and hoped to fit in among the leaders of his day. His clothes were elegant. He spoke clearly and was serious and **conservative** in both his manner and opinions. Fillmore left behind his country habits in the same way he replaced his rough cowhide boots with polished leather shoes. Although his law work was not brilliant or showy, it was accurate and won him many court cases. Fellow lawyers and Buffalo's leaders began saying, "If Millard Fillmore goes for it, so do I."

In 1823, Fillmore left Buffalo to practice law in the small town of East Aurora, where his parents lived. By opening an office in a small community, he could get more experience. Fillmore was modest, and his achievements in Buffalo had not gone to his head.

With his law practice established, he married Abigail Powers on February 5, 1826. Her faith in his abilities encouraged him. She knew about the social graces of the day. She knew which fork to use at the dinner table, which clothes to wear, and which people were important to meet. Her manners helped him move further away from his backwoods past. This final polish to his image led to his entry into **politics.** In 1828, the same year that their son, Millard Powers Fillmore, was born, the lawyer from East Aurora was elected to the New York State Assembly. He had the backing of the Anti-Mason **political party.** The Anti-Mason Party had formed to oppose the Masons, a secret society, which some people thought had grown too powerful.

Until the 1830s, there were no "left" and "right" shoes. All shoes and boots were cut on straight "lasts." Shoes had to be broken in to be comfortable.

THE ANTI-MASONS

Political parties in the first half of the 19th century were nothing like political parties today. Often, a single cause or belief could evolve into a political party. The Anti-Masons were organized to combat the Ancient Order of Masons, also known as the Freemasons. The Ancient Order of the Masons is a secret society that was founded in 1717 in London, England. The Masons' rituals are kept secret from nonmembers. To become a member, a man must be elected by other members. Women are not allowed to become Masons. A Masonic ritual is depicted in the illustration above, and Masonic symbols are shown in the illustration to the right.

The Masons were originally formed to promote religious and moral ideas. But Anti-Masons believed the organization was an "invisible empire." They thought the organization had gained too much power in the United States because many important men belonged to it.

A Mason named William Morgan threatened to tell the order's secrets. In 1826, he was kidnapped and no one ever saw him again. The Anti-Masons claimed that the Masons had murdered him. No one was ever convicted of his murder, though three men were convicted of his kidnapping. Anti-Masons said the organization got away with murder because it was so powerful.

Although many famous men (including President George Washington) had been Masons, newspapers and churches fueled the Anti-Masons' claims. Fillmore distrusted any organization that put itself beyond the rule of the law, as the Masons had done. He joined forces with the Anti-Masons. The single goal of the Anti-Masons—to destroy the Masonic Order—was not strong enough to maintain a political party. By 1834, the party had disbanded. Most Anti-Masons joined either the Whig or the Democratic parties.

CHAPTER TWO

A MAN OF HIS TIME

F illmore was quiet and attentive during his first term in the New York State Assembly. This style of watching and waiting was a holdover from his early years of learning new trades while working for demanding bosses. While learning to be an assembly-man, it worked to his advantage.

After Fillmore was reelected in 1830, he took on more responsibility. He submitted a **bill** to keep people who could not pay their debts from being thrown in jail. It passed in 1831. Always working for the "weak and unprotected," Fillmore was in favor of any increase in business that would provide more jobs. At the time, people and goods were usually transported on boats. People dug canals to create waterways across land. This made transportation from place to place both easier and faster. Fillmore backed bills to improve canals or dig new ones. In a short time, Fillmore had become a force in New York politics.

Millard Fillmore's style of quiet leadership fol-lowed him into private life in Buffalo, when he left the assembly in 1831. The family entered into Buffalo's social, **civic,** and political life. Fillmore helped draw

up Buffalo's city **charter.** He saw to the creation of an organized fire-fighting system. The Fillmores enjoyed associating with Buffalo's elite. In 1832, Abigail Fillmore gave birth to their daughter, Mary Abigail.

By the end of that year, Millard Fillmore was ready to enter national politics. He was elected to the U.S. Congress that year with the backing of the Anti-Mason Party. By this time, the Anti-Mason Party was losing support. Fillmore urged them to disband and join the new Whig Party. The Whig Party had formed to oppose President Andrew Jackson.

William Rickaby Miller made this painting of the Erie Canal. Fillmore believed that building canals would help New York's economy.

General Andrew Jackson (on white horse) led U.S. forces in the Battle of New Orleans. The American victory in the battle made Jackson a hero.

Called "Old Hickory," Andrew Jackson enjoyed a reputation as a tough warrior. In the War of 1812, Jackson had gathered a mixed force of regular soldiers, pirates, frontiersmen, Indians, and freed black slaves to defend New Orleans against British forces. Jackson's men fought from behind cotton bales and mud barricades. They held their fire until the British soldiers marched into view with bagpipes blaring and drums thundering. The battle was short and sharp. By its end, Jackson's ragtag army had defeated a much larger

British force. Unfortunately, the same stubborn bravery that made Jackson a good soldier did not make him a good politician. His years as president were riddled with economic and financial upheaval.

Fillmore was quiet and observant during his first term in Congress, just as he had been when he entered the New York State Assembly. He gathered information by closely watching the actions of other lawmakers. He returned to private life in 1835 after serving only one term in the house. But after a year spent in New York, he ran for office again. He was reelected to Congress in 1836.

The Battle of New Orleans happened two weeks after a **treaty** was signed in Belgium ending the War of 1812. Word of the signing had not reached the United States in time to stop the fight.

Millard Fillmore was considered a careful and trustworthy man. This reputation made him popular among New York voters.

Millard Fillmore's
uncle, Jesse Millard,
was a Mason.

The Whig Party was
made up of people
from other parties
who had one thing
in common: they
opposed President
Andrew Jackson.
The party existed
from the mid-1830s,
when Fillmore joined,
until about 1854.

In time, Fillmore became a powerful figure in Congress. In 1842, he backed a high **tariff,** or tax, on foreign goods brought into the United States. High tariffs made U.S. products cheaper than foreign ones. But President John Tyler, like many southerners, supported low tariffs. Few goods were manufactured in the South. It was instead a farming region, and southerners had long relied on buying less expensive goods from Europe. Fillmore figured out a way to get the tariff passed. He delayed votes on the tariff bill until the government was so desperate for money that it needed the tariff payments. President Tyler had no choice but to sign the high-tariff bill into law.

Usually, there were more Democrats in Congress than Whigs. The Whigs had to fight to get their laws passed. They sometimes had a difficult time making their opinions known because Democrats refused to let them have their say. Fillmore angrily challenged the Democrats, saying, "I speak by right, and not by permission! I will never . . . yield a right . . . guaranteed by the **Constitution.**"

In 1843, Fillmore departed Congress once again—this time to run for New York State governor in the 1844 election. He was beaten because many **immigrants** in New York City voted against the Whigs. Many people who were born in the United States feared they would lose their jobs to the waves of foreigners who were pouring into the country. The Whigs were "**nativist.**" They believed "native" Americans—those who had been born in the United

States and were already working in government and business—should run the country. They wanted immigrants to hold only the lowest paying jobs. In fact, they did their best to stop immigration altogether.

In 1847, Fillmore was elected to the powerful job of state comptroller. The comptroller controlled the spending of New York's money. Millard and Abigail moved to Albany, the state capital. They sent their son to Harvard Law School and enrolled their daughter in a Massachusetts school for young ladies. Fillmore would not stay out of national politics for long, however. The scramble for control of the **federal** government would soon pull him back to Washington, D.C.

General Zachary Taylor became a hero during the Mexican-American War, which the United States and Mexico fought between 1846 and 1848. Taylor owned a **plantation** and slaves, which made him popular with Whigs from the southern states. The Whigs **nominated** Taylor as their presidential **candidate.** Now the party needed to find a candidate for vice president who would please Whigs in the northern part of the United States who opposed slavery.

Fillmore's son, Millard Powers Fillmore, served as his father's assistant in Washington, D.C.

Millard Fillmore was a temperate man. He neither smoked nor drank alcohol. He only gambled once in his life, at age 15, when he entered a raffle and won a turkey on New Year's Day.

All attention turned to Millard Fillmore, and soon he was nominated to run with Taylor. The Whig **ticket** of Taylor and Fillmore won the 1848 election by a small number of votes. Once again, Fillmore packed his belongings for the move to Washington. This time, Abigail was very ill and did not go with him. He would be without her advice and support as he started the most important job thus far in his successful career.

This poster shows Zachary Taylor and Millard Fillmore, the Whig Party candidates for president and vice president in 1848.

THE MEXICAN-AMERICAN WAR

In 1845, the U.S. government claimed Texas as part of the Union. The United States hoped to claim California as well. The conflict was driven by the idea of Manifest Destiny, the belief that God intended Americans to spread across North America.

On January 1, 1846, American troops under General Zachary Taylor crossed into Mexico. Several skirmishes followed in the coming months, and in May the war officially began. The Americans hoped to take Veracruz, on Mexico's east coast, and then head inland toward Mexico City. General Winfield Scott and 12,000 American soldiers landed 3 miles southeast of Veracruz on March 9, 1847. After gaining control of the city, they began their march toward the Mexican capital. The Americans bombarded Mexico City and eventually captured the city. The painting above shows General Scott's troops entering Mexico City.

The Treaty of Guadalupe Hidalgo, which ended the war, gave the United States the land that would become the states of New Mexico, Nevada, Utah, Arizona, and California. By helping win the war, General Zachary Taylor became a great American hero.

CHAPTER THREE

"ZACHARY TAYLOR IS NO MORE"

With the Whig's victory in the election of 1848, Fillmore stepped into a political whirlwind. Being Zachary Taylor's vice president was not easy for Fillmore. Before the **inauguration,** he and Taylor had been together in formal functions, and Taylor had been pleasant enough. But once they were actually in office, the new president became distant. Fillmore found himself cut off from the president by a gang of scheming politicians who wanted important government jobs for their **cronies.** By the time Fillmore realized what had happened, he had to wait until Congress was in session before he could do anything about it. But by then, Congress had bigger problems to deal with.

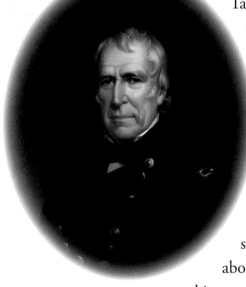

Zachary Taylor in 1848

The Senate was equally divided between states that allowed slavery and states that outlawed it. The new **territory** won in the Mexican-American War

threatened to upset that balance. California's new constitution banned slavery, so southern congressmen rejected any bill including that territory. Northern **abolitionists** wanted slavery banned in all the new territories.

According to the U.S. Constitution, the vice president **presides** over the Senate. If a vote ends in a tie, the vice president gets to vote, breaking the tie. It appeared that the bills concerning slavery might stall with a tie. Fillmore knew he may very well have to cast the deciding vote. His northern supporters clamored for him to take their side, while the southern states threatened to leave the Union and form their own country. Fillmore was torn.

Millard Fillmore was caught in the middle of the national argument over slavery. In this illustration, Fillmore (center) is shown trying to stop a fight between a slaveholder and an abolitionist.

During the presidential **campaign,** Fillmore had said that he was against the slavery of any human being. But he also believed the states, not the federal government, should decide whether to allow slavery. He said he regarded "slavery as an evil, but one with which the National Government had nothing to do."

Senator Henry Clay proposed a **compromise** in January 1850. California would be admitted as a free state in which slavery would not be permitted. New Mexico and Utah would be established as territories

Congressmen from the North and South bitterly debated whether to allow slavery in the territories. Senator Henry Clay (standing in center) proposed the Compromise of 1850, which he hoped would settle the issue.

24

and be allowed to make their own decisions about slavery. Clay's compromise also dealt with the slave market that operated in Washington, D.C. It stated that the slave trade would no longer be allowed in the nation's capital. Finally, the federal government would firmly enforce the Fugitive Slave Act of 1793. This act stated that any slaves who escaped to the North had to be returned to their southern masters. Clay's ideas became known as the Compromise of 1850. Senators argued angrily over the compromise.

Fillmore was in a bad position. He did not want to cast the tie-breaking vote. As June 1850 approached, tempers were as hot as the summer weather that drove many congressmen from the capital city. President Taylor was against the compromise bill. He threatened a **veto** if the Senate passed it. The Senate was in a panic. Everyone was waiting to see how Fillmore would vote.

Fillmore never cast that ballot as vice president because around this time, President Taylor became ill. Instead of resting, Taylor had celebrated Independence Day in the capital. At one gala event on the hot day, the president ate a number of servings of iced milk, cold cherries, and pickled cucumbers. Later, he developed stomach cramps.

At noon on July 9, 1850, Fillmore was in the Senate chamber when a messenger informed him that President Taylor was seriously ill. Fillmore visited the president at the White House and then went to his apartment at Willard's Hotel. A messenger brought a

Even though they were running on the same ticket, Fillmore did not meet Zachary Taylor until after they won the election of 1848.

During his vice presidency, Fillmore lived in a room at Willard's Hotel. His wife was ill at the time and preferred to stay in New York.

Slaves were bought and sold at markets like the one depicted in this painting. As part of the Compromise of 1850, the slave market in Washington, D.C., was closed. Slavery was still allowed in the capital, but enslaved people could no longer be bought and sold there.

note late that evening. There were many words on it, but Fillmore could only see the important ones: "Sir, . . . Zachary Taylor, late President of the United States is no more."

With the death of the president, Vice President Fillmore took over. He was sworn in as the 13th president of the United States on July 10, 1850. He gave no speech at the inauguration. "Neither the time nor the occasion appeared to require [it]," said Fillmore. "The country was shrouded in . . . grief."

Fillmore did not sleep that night. His place in U.S. history depended on his next actions, and he was nervous. After heated discussions, the Senate accepted most parts of Henry Clay's compromise bill. California became a state. Utah and New Mexico became territories and would decide their own slavery questions. Washington's slave market was closed. A stronger Fugitive Slave Act was passed. When President Fillmore signed the new act, it angered those who wanted to see slavery ended. He saw it as an act of compromise to save the Union from a **civil war.** His northern supporters saw it as a betrayal.

Fillmore believed that both sides had misunderstood him. "In the North I was charged with being a pro-slavery man, seeking to extend slavery over free territory," he wrote, "and in the South I was accused of being an abolitionist. But I am neither." He had simply done what he believed was best for the Union.

On October 23, 1850, Fillmore wrote to Daniel Webster, one of his advisers. "God knows that I detest slavery," wrote Fillmore, "but it is an existing evil, for which we [the present government] are not responsible, and we must endure it, and give it protection as is guaranteed by the Constitution 'til we can get rid of it without destroying the last hope of free government in the world."

While trying to calm the North-South conflict, Fillmore also tried to be an effective president. His son became his secretary. His beautiful daughter and frail wife guided the social life at the White House. Always avid readers, Millard and Abigail Fillmore installed the first library in the White House. President Fillmore

Millard Fillmore was one of eight vice presidents who became president when the elected president died.

Fillmore was the last president from the Whig Party. The party fell apart shortly after his presidency.

approved a plan for Matthew Perry of the U.S. Navy to sail a small fleet to Japan. He hoped that the voyage would open Japan to American trade. In 1853, Perry sailed into the formerly closed port of Yeddo (now Tokyo) and began to **negotiate** an agreement. During his time, Fillmore also proposed a transcontinental railroad, which was finally completed in 1869.

Fillmore had a vision for the United States. Future presidents acted on many of his ideas. His party did not nominate him to run in the next presidential election, so his time as president came to an end. In the 1852 election, Democrat Franklin Pierce defeated General Winfield Scott, the Whig candidate. The Whig Party was finished.

Millard Fillmore's daughter, Mary, was born in 1832.

CHAPTER FOUR

RETURN TO BUFFALO

With his presidency behind him, Fillmore looked forward to returning to a peaceful, relaxing life in his home town of Buffalo, New York. He wanted to forget the stormy political battles he had weathered in Washington.

But before he could say goodbye to the capital city for good, Franklin Pierce had to be inaugurated as president. The weather during his inauguration was terribly cold. Despite the bitter wind, Millard and Abigail Fillmore stood by to honor the new president at the outdoor ceremony. Unfortunately, Abigail caught a cold that quickly turned into pneumonia. She died later that month on March 30, 1853. Brokenhearted, Fillmore returned to Buffalo. A year later, tragedy struck again. His daughter, Mary, died at age 22 after a sudden illness. The loss of his beloved wife and daughter crushed Fillmore.

Nonetheless, he continued to work for the good of his city. He helped found Buffalo General Hospital in 1855. He also became involved with a new political party called the "Know-Nothings." This group was officially known as the American Party. It grew out of the anti-immigrant nativist movement of the 1840s. Although the American Party members were not strictly against immigration, they wanted to restrict the rights of newcomers. They did not believe immigrants should have the right to vote or hold public office. They also favored a 21-year waiting period before immigrants could become U.S. citizens.

The nativists were particularly opposed to Catholic immigrants. Here, an anti-Catholic mob attacks troops in Philadelphia.

THE MAN WHO WAS "AGAINST"

Millard Fillmore had a single overarching flaw during his career as a politician. He chose to join organizations that were "against" rather than "for" important issues. The Anti-Mason Party that supported Fillmore for his first public office in 1828 battled to end the Ancient Order of Masons, a powerful secret society that counted many famous men among its members. This single issue was not strong enough in its appeal to the public to hold together a political party.

Next, he joined the Whig Party. It, too, had one purpose: to defeat Andrew Jackson in his campaign for the presidency. While the Whigs held together for 24 years, they were usually a minority in Congress and collapsed after the end of Fillmore's presidency.

Finally, he joined the American Party—the Know-Nothings. They were against immigrants' rights. Instead, they favored people who had been born in the United States. The American Party dissolved after James Buchanan defeated Fillmore for president in 1856.

Whigs parade through New York. Fillmore was first a Whig and then a Know-Nothing. Both groups were hostile to immigrants.

Fillmore's anti-immigrant feelings had grown firmer when immigrants in New York City voted against him in the 1844 election for governor. So when the American Party asked him to run for president in the 1856 election, he accepted. He had been in Europe for a year, but he returned on June 22 to a fireworks reception as his ship docked in New York. The Know-Nothings had a 50-gun salute fired in his honor. Crowds followed the former president home to Buffalo, where his campaign began. His main message to the American people was consistent. "When I left the Presidential chair, the whole nation was prosperous and contented," he said. "But where are we now? Alas! threatened at home with civil war!"

During the summer of 1856, the Know-Nothings lost their early drive and drama. They tried to rally around their weak slogan, "America should be governed by Americans." But the passions had dwindled.

Democrat James Buchanan defeated Fillmore and Republican candidate John C. Frémont to become the 15th president.

Fillmore retired from political life. In 1858, he married Caroline McIntosh, a wealthy widow. During the Civil War, he supported Buffalo's volunteer soldiers and the Union cause. But he strongly criticized Abraham Lincoln and the Republican Party. He said they were too quick to go to war. He thought the North and South should have tried to negotiate first. Still, Fillmore

When people asked members of the American Party about its ideas and goals, they often responded by saying, "I know nothing." They wanted to keep their ideas secret. People began calling them the "Know-Nothing" Party.

In 1858, Millard Fillmore bought this elegant mansion in Buffalo. He would live there for the rest of his life.

To show his support for the Union during the Civil War, Fillmore organized a company of men who were too old to join the army. Wearing uniforms of their own design, these men helped raise money for the war effort.

Fillmore disagreed with Abraham Lincoln over how to handle the tensions between the North and the South. But after winning the 1860 election, Lincoln stopped in Buffalo on his way to Washington, D.C. Fillmore spent a friendly weekend with Lincoln and invited him to dinner at his home.

stood firm with his country. At a meeting in Buffalo, he said, "My fellow citizens, it is no time for any man to shrink from the responsibility which events have cast upon him. We have reached a crisis . . . when no man . . . has the right to stand **neutral.**"

Many of his enemies accused him of **treason** when he did not support President Lincoln. As long as he lived, Fillmore stood by what he believed.

In February 1874, Fillmore suffered a stroke. On March 8, a second stroke killed him. Fillmore was truly an American of his time. He pulled himself up from his life as a poor farmer's son to become the vice president of the United States. He served as U.S. president for two difficult years while critics in northern states called him a **traitor** for signing the Fugitive Slave Act. As the United States stood at the brink of civil war, he tried to preserve the Union. He lost his career in politics as he attempted to hold the nation together. Throughout his career, Millard Fillmore was a respected leader and a master of compromise.

When Fillmore visited England in 1855, Oxford University offered him a special degree to honor his success, even though he had never attended college. Fillmore refused to accept the honor because he felt he had "neither literary nor scientific attainment."

Caroline McIntosh married Millard Fillmore in 1858.

THE BUFFALO
HISTORICAL SOCIETY

During the spring of 1862, Buffalo citizens wanted to find a way
to protect the "relics and records" of the city's colorful past. They
approached Millard Fillmore to enlist his talent for organization.
Less than 30 days later, the Buffalo Historical Society was
founded. Fillmore became its first president. He threw himself
into the work. At the society's opening ceremonies, he said,
"the object of this society [was] not to study history . . . or the
formation of a library for that purpose; but its chief object is to
collect and preserve materials of history relating to western New
York, and especially to Buffalo, for future use."

This limited goal was abandoned in a short time. Fillmore found himself both studying and teaching Buffalo history as the museum expanded. The society grew rapidly from its location at 7 Court Street (left), leasing rooms in other locations. Eventually, the St. James Hotel in downtown Buffalo was remodeled to house the Buffalo Historical Society, the Fine Arts Academy, and the Society of Natural Sciences. Three of Fillmore's favorite institutions were now under one roof.

T I M E   L I N E

1800	1810	1820	1830	1840

1800
Millard Fillmore is born on January 7 in a log cabin in Cayuga County, New York.

1814
Fillmore becomes an apprentice at a cloth mill.

1819
Fillmore meets Abigail Powers, his future wife.

1822
Fillmore moves to Buffalo, New York, where he works as a teacher and a law clerk.

1823
Fillmore opens a law office in East Aurora, New York.

1826
Fillmore and Abigail Powers are married.

1828
The Fillmores' son, Millard Powers Fillmore, is born. Fillmore is elected to the New York legislature.

1832
The Fillmores' daughter, Mary Abigail, is born. Fillmore is elected to the U.S. Congress.

1835
Fillmore leaves Congress and returns to practicing law.

1836
Fillmore runs for Congress again and is reelected.

1843
Fillmore runs for governor of New York. He loses the election, in part because of the Whig Party's anti-immigrant stance.

1846
The United States goes to war with Mexico.

1847
Fillmore is elected New York comptroller. In September, the United States captures Mexico City. Mexico is forced to surrender.

1848

The Mexican-American War ends with the signing of the Treaty of Guadalupe Hidalgo. The Whig Party nominates war hero Zachary Taylor as its presidential candidate. The party decides to find a northerner to run for vice president in an attempt to gain more votes. They nominate Fillmore. In November, Taylor and Fillmore win the election.

1849

Zachary Taylor is inaugurated as the 12th U.S. president on March 4. Millard Fillmore becomes vice president.

1850

President Taylor dies in July after a brief illness. Fillmore becomes the 13th U.S. president. President Fillmore agrees to the Compromise of 1850 to help preserve the Union. By supporting the compromise, he offends people on both sides of the slavery issue. The Compromise of 1850 admits California to the Union as a free state. New Mexico, Utah, and Arizona become territories.

1851

President Fillmore proposes Commodore Matthew Perry's voyage to open trade with Japan. Perry does not set sail until 1853.

1852

The Whig Party turns its back on Millard Fillmore and nominates General Winfield Scott as its presidential candidate. The Whigs lose the election, and the party falls apart.

1853

Franklin Pierce is inaugurated as the 14th U.S. president. Abigail Powers Fillmore attends the inauguration with her husband, even though the weather is terrible. She catches a cold and dies of pneumonia. Fillmore returns to private life in Buffalo.

1854

Fillmore's daughter, Mary Abigail Fillmore, dies suddenly at age 22.

1855

Fillmore helps fund and build the Buffalo General Hospital.

1856

Fillmore runs for president as the "Know-Nothing" Party candidate. He loses the election to James Buchanan.

1858

Fillmore marries Caroline McIntosh, a wealthy widow. They purchase a mansion in Buffalo and frequently host parties.

1861

Fillmore supports the Civil War but is critical of Abraham Lincoln. To prove his support for the Union cause, Fillmore organizes a company of men who are too old to fight in the war. The group calls itself the "Union Continentals."

1862

Fillmore helps found the Buffalo Historical Society.

1867

Fillmore founds the Buffalo Society for Prevention of Cruelty to Animals.

1874

Millard Fillmore dies of a stroke on March 8.

GLOSSARY

abolitionists (ab-uh-LISH-uh-nists)
Abolitionists were people who wanted to end slavery in the United States. Northern abolitionists felt that Fillmore did not do enough to end slavery.

apprentice (uh-PREN-tiss) An apprentice is a person who is learning a skill under the teaching of an expert worker. In Fillmore's time, an apprentice agreed to work for very low pay for a promised length of time.

bill (BILL) A bill is a proposed law presented to a group of people who make laws. Congress and the president decide if bills become laws.

campaign (kam-PAYN) A campaign is the process of running for an election, including activities such as giving speeches or attending rallies. The Whig Party wanted to defeat Andrew Jackson in his campaign for the presidency.

candidate (KAN-duh-dayt) A candidate is a person who is running in an election. At least two candidates run for president every four years.

charter (CHAR-tur) A charter is a written statement that grants certain rights to people or a group. Fillmore helped write the charter for the city of Buffalo.

civic (SIV-ik) Civic means having to do with a city. Fillmore was interested in Buffalo's civic affairs.

civil war (SIV-il WAR) A civil war is a war between opposing groups of citizens within the same nation. Fillmore hoped the Compromise of 1850 would prevent a civil war.

compromise (KOM-pruh-myz) A compromise is a way to settle a disagreement in which both sides give up part of what they want. The U.S. Senate created the Compromise of 1850 in an attempt to satisfy both the North and the South.

conservative (kun-SER-vuh-tiv) If someone is conservative, he or she is cautious and prefers not to take risks. Fillmore was considered a serious and conservative man.

constitution (kon-stih-TOO-shun) A constitution is the set of basic principles that govern a state, country, or society. California's constitution outlawed slavery.

cronies (KROH-neez) Cronies are old friends of a politician who are given government jobs regardless of their qualifications. Early in President Taylor's term, some politicians made sure their cronies were appointed to important jobs.

federal (FED-ur-ul) Federal means having to do with the central government of the United States, rather than a state or city government. Fillmore believed that individual states, not the federal government, should decide whether to permit or ban slavery.

immigrants (IM-uh-grunts) Immigrants are people who move to a new country. New York City had a large population of immigrants during Fillmore's time.

inauguration (ih-naw-gyuh-RAY-shun) An inauguration is the ceremony that takes place when a new president begins a term of office. Abigail Fillmore became seriously ill after Franklin Pierce's inauguration.

nativist (NAY-tuh-vist) A nativist was someone who believed that immigrants should not be allowed to vote in elections or hold public office. Fillmore became a nativist after he lost an election because of a strong immigrant vote.

negotiate (ni-GOH-she-ayt) If people negotiate, they talk things over and try to come to an agreement. Commodore Perry sailed to Japan to negotiate a trade agreement.

neutral (NOO-trul) If people are neutral, they do not take sides. Fillmore believed that no one should remain neutral during the Civil War.

nominated (NOM-uh-nayt-ed) When someone is nominated, he or she is chosen to run for office. The Whigs nominated Fillmore to be their candidate for vice president.

plantation (plan-TAY-shun) A plantation is a large farm that grows crops such as tobacco, sugarcane, or cotton. Zachary Taylor was a plantation owner and a slaveholder.

political party (puh-LIT-uh-kul PAR-tee) A political party is a group of people who share similar ideas about how to run a government. The Whig political party was a group of people that joined forces to oppose President Andrew Jackson.

politics (PAWL-uh-tiks) Politics refers to the actions and practices of the government. Millard Fillmore's first job in politics was as a member of the New York State Assembly.

presides (preh-ZYDZ) If someone presides over a meeting, he or she is in charge of it and must keep order during discussions. The vice president presides over the Senate.

tariff (TAYR-iff) A tariff is a tax charged on goods brought in from other countries. The southern states used many products from overseas and wanted to keep tariffs low.

territory (TAYR-uh-tor-ee) A territory is a land or region, especially land that belongs to a government. Utah and New Mexico were made territories of the United States.

ticket (TIK-it) In an election, a ticket is the list of candidates from the same political party who are running for office. Zachary Taylor and Millard Fillmore were running on the Whig ticket.

traitor (TRAY-tur) A traitor is a person who betrays his or her country. People said Fillmore was a traitor when he signed the Fugitive Slave Act.

treason (TREE-zun) Treason is the act of hurting one's country or helping its enemies. People accused Fillmore of treason when he refused to support President Lincoln.

treaty (TREE-tee) A treaty is a formal agreement between nations. Mexico was forced to accept the terms of the Treaty of Guadalupe Hidalgo in 1848.

union (YOON-yen) A union is the joining together of two or more people or groups of people, such as states. The United States is also known as the Union.

veto (VEE-toh) A veto is the president's power to refuse to sign a bill into law. President Zachary Taylor threatened to veto the bill that became the Compromise of 1850.

THE UNITED STATES GOVERNMENT

The United States government is divided into three equal branches: the executive, the legislative, and the judicial. This division helps prevent abuses of power because each branch has to answer to the other two. No one branch can become too powerful.

EXECUTIVE BRANCH

PRESIDENT
VICE PRESIDENT
DEPARTMENTS

The job of the executive branch is to enforce the laws. It is headed by the president, who serves as the spokesperson for the United States around the world. The president signs bills into law and appoints important officials such as federal judges. He or she is also the commander in chief of the U.S. military. The president is assisted by the vice president, who takes over if the president dies or cannot carry out the duties of the office.

The executive branch also includes various departments, each focused on a specific topic. They include the Defense Department, the Justice Department, and the Agriculture Department. The department heads, along with other officials such as the vice president, serve as the president's closest advisers, called the cabinet.

LEGISLATIVE BRANCH

CONGRESS
Senate and
House of Representatives

The job of the legislative branch is to make the laws. It consists of Congress, which is divided into two parts: the Senate and the House of Representatives. The Senate has 100 members, and the House of Representatives has 435 members. Each state has two senators. The number of representatives a state has varies depending on the state's population.

Besides making laws, Congress also passes budgets and enacts taxes. In addition, it is responsible for declaring war, maintaining the military, and regulating trade with other countries.

JUDICIAL BRANCH

SUPREME COURT
COURTS OF APPEALS
DISTRICT COURTS

The job of the judicial branch is to interpret the laws. It consists of the nation's federal courts. Trials are held in district courts. During trials, judges must decide what laws mean and how they apply. Courts of appeals review the decisions made in district courts.

The nation's highest court is the Supreme Court. If someone disagrees with a court of appeals ruling, he or she can ask the Supreme Court to review it. The Supreme Court may refuse. The Supreme Court makes sure that decisions and laws do not violate the Constitution.

CHOOSING
THE PRESIDENT

It may seem odd, but American voters don't elect the president directly. Instead, the president is chosen using what is called the Electoral College.

Each state gets as many votes in the Electoral College as its combined total of senators and representatives in Congress. For example, Iowa has two senators and five representatives, so it gets seven electoral votes. Although the District of Columbia does not have any voting members in Congress, it gets three electoral votes. Usually, the candidate who wins the most votes in any given state receives all of that state's electoral votes.

To become president, a candidate must get more than half of the Electoral College votes. There are a total of 538 votes in the Electoral College, so a candidate needs 270 votes to win. If nobody receives 270 Electoral College votes, the House of Representatives chooses the president.

With the Electoral College system, the person who receives the most votes nationwide does not always receive the most electoral votes. This happened most recently in 2000, when Al Gore received half a million more national votes than George W. Bush. Bush became president because he had more Electoral College votes.

THE WHITE HOUSE

The White House is the official home of the president of the United States. It is located at 1600 Pennsylvania Avenue NW in Washington, D.C. In 1792, a contest was held to select the architect who would design the president's home. James Hoban won. Construction took eight years.

The first president, George Washington, never lived in the White House. The second president, John Adams, moved into the house in 1800, though the inside was not yet complete. During the War of 1812, British soldiers burned down much of the White House. It was rebuilt several years later.

The White House was changed through the years. Porches were added, and President Theodore Roosevelt added the West Wing. President William Taft changed the shape of the presidential office, making it into the famous Oval Office. While Harry Truman was president, the old house was discovered to be structurally weak. All the walls were reinforced with steel, and the rooms were rebuilt.

Today, the White House has 132 rooms (including 35 bathrooms), 28 fireplaces, and 3 elevators. It takes 570 gallons of paint to cover the outside of the six-story building. The White House provides the president with many ways to relax. It includes a putting green, a jogging track, a swimming pool, a tennis court, and beautifully landscaped gardens. The White House also has a movie theater, a billiard room, and a one-lane bowling alley.

PRESIDENTIAL PERKS

The job of president of the United States is challenging. It is probably one of the most stressful jobs in the world. Because of this, presidents are paid well, though not nearly as well as the leaders of large corporations. In 2007, the president earned $400,000 a year. Presidents also receive extra benefits that make the demanding job a little more appealing.

★ **Camp David:** In the 1940s, President Franklin D. Roosevelt chose this heavily wooded spot in the mountains of Maryland to be the presidential retreat, where presidents can relax. Even though it is a retreat, world business is conducted there. Most famously, President Jimmy Carter met with Middle Eastern leaders at Camp David in 1978. The result was a peace agreement between Israel and Egypt.

★ *Air Force One:* The president flies on a jet called *Air Force One*. It is a Boeing 747-200B that has been modified to meet the president's needs.

Air Force One is the size of a large home. It is equipped with a dining room, sleeping quarters, a conference room, and office space. It also has two kitchens that can provide food for up to 50 people.

★ **The Secret Service:** While not the most glamorous of the president's perks, the Secret Service is one of the most important. The Secret Service is a group of highly trained agents who protect the president and the president's family.

★ **The Presidential State Car:** The presidential limousine is a stretch Cadillac DTS.

It has been armored to protect the president in case of attack. Inside the plush car are a foldaway desk, an entertainment center, and a communications console.

★ **The Food:** The White House has five chefs who will make any food the president wants. The White House also has an extensive wine collection.

★ **Retirement:** A former president receives a pension, or retirement pay, of just under $180,000 a year. Former presidents also receive Secret Service protection for the rest of their lives.

FACTS

QUALIFICATIONS

To run for president, a candidate must

* be at least 35 years old
* be a citizen who was born in the United States
* have lived in the United States for 14 years

TERM OF OFFICE

A president's term of office is four years.
No president can stay in office for more than two terms.

ELECTION DATE

The presidential election takes place every four years on the first Tuesday of November.

INAUGURATION DATE

Presidents are inaugurated on January 20.

OATH OF OFFICE

I do solemnly swear I will faithfully execute the office of the President of the United States and will to the best of my ability preserve, protect, and defend the Constitution of the United States.

WRITE A LETTER TO THE PRESIDENT

One of the best things about being a U.S. citizen is that Americans get to participate in their government. They can speak out if they feel government leaders aren't doing their jobs. They can also praise leaders who are going the extra mile. Do you have something you'd like the president to do? Should the president worry more about the environment and encourage people to recycle? Should the government spend more money on our schools? You can write a letter to the president to say how you feel!

1600 Pennsylvania Avenue
Washington, D.C. 20500
You can even send an e-mail to: president@whitehouse.gov

Books

Carey, Charles W., Jr. *The Mexican War: Mr. Polk's War.* Berkeley Heights, NJ: Enslow Publishers, 2002.

Cleveland, Will, and Mark Alvarez. *Yo Millard Fillmore (And All Those Other Presidents You Don't Know).* Brookfield, CT: Millbrook Press, 1999.

Collier, Christopher. *Slavery and the Coming of the Civil War, 1831–1861.* New York: Benchmark Books, 2000.

Santella, Andrew. *Millard Fillmore.* Minneapolis: Compass Point Books, 2003.

Santow, Dan. *Millard Fillmore: America's 13th President.* New York: Children's Press, 2004.

Souter, Gerry, and Janet Souter. *The Founding of the United States Experience.* London: Presidio Press, 2006.

Videos

The American President. DVD (Hollywood, CA: PBS Paramount, 2000).

The History Channel Presents The Presidents. DVD (New York: A&E Home Video, 2005).

Internet Sites

Visit our Web page for lots of links about Millard Fillmore and other U.S. presidents:

http://www.childsworld.com/links

Note to Parents, Teachers, and Librarians: We routinely verify our Web links to make sure they are safe, active sites—so encourage your readers to check them out!

For More Information

INDEX